AF879729

Your True Order

Guide to Gathering, Organizing and Storing Your Personal Records

O. Escobar

Your True Order
Guide to Gathering, Organizing and Storing Your Personal Records

Copyright © 2017 by Olga M. Escobar

Cover Art by: O. Escobar © 2017 Olga M. Escobar
Painting Title: No. 35 – Mi Angel Ella

All Rights Reserved.

No part of this book may be used, reproduced, scanned, or distributed in any matter whatsoever without written permission from the author except in the case of brief quotations embodied in critical articles and reviews. Reproduction prohibitions do not apply to forms contained in this product when reproduced for personal use.

The eBook and printable PDF is licensed for your personal use only. The eBook and printable PDF may not be resold or given away to other people.

For information contact:

O. Escobar /Your True Order
PO Box 47022
Windsor Mill, MD 21244
www.oescobar.org

Printed in the United States of America.
First Printing, October 2017

ISBN-13: 978-0-9994468-0-5
ISBN-13: 978-0-9994468-1-2 (eBook)

Dedication

Dear Reader

Do not fear the chaos — embrace your true order.

Contents

Authors Note

We are the center of our own universe. Our multitasking life includes trying to be a full-time everything. We work full time, take care of our home, our children, aging parents, and maybe a beloved pet. We are responsible for all the 'paperwork,' e.g. bills, birth certificates, passports, insurance and finances. We are also responsible for knowing and remembering passwords, pin numbers, and login information.

As the center of our own universe, we live an autonomous life. Every day we make personal choices and financial decisions that matter. Many of us have a great handle on our finances, but our record keeping systems might not be obvious to family members, advisors or friends who might need immediate access to them in times of emergency. Would your loved ones be able to quickly locate your important information or know how to handle your affairs?

Since my answer was a resounding No, I created Your True Order. A guide that outlines what vital information you need to gather, then organize, and store — so that it can be conveniently and safely accessed — then shared, when needed, with appropriate individuals.

I encourage you to be good to yourself and those who love you by investing the time to create Your True Order.

Preface

Benjamin Franklin wrote, "In this world nothing can be said to be certain, except death and taxes." The less animated side of "certainty" includes the billions of unclaimed bank accounts and other assets currently held by State treasurers instead of beloved family, friends, or a charity — all because of unfilled and unsought paperwork.

The Your True Order guide is a preventative method to protect yourself and your assets against the misfortunes and inopportune disasters that inevitably play a role in our lives. By completing the tedious but necessary paperwork, creating multiple backups, and utilizing this guide to create a system where your vital information is accessible, you will lift the additional burden of "what now" should a disaster occur.

Gathering, organizing and providing access to your important personal and financial information, and documents, is one of the best gifts you can give yourself and those you love.

Introduction

The process of knowing what important personal information and documents you need to gather, and then knowing how to organize the information can be overwhelming. The Your True Order guide offers effective strategies, practical solutions, and organized long-term result to store and decrypt your personal and financial decisions, should others need access to your vital information.

The **Your True Order Guide (YTO), Workbook** and **Checklist** will ease the process for you. The three-prong approach will help you acknowledge, assemble and provide access into your universe. How it works:

- The **YTO Guide** will help you to identify and gather your essential information from a personal, legal and financial perspective. The YTO Guide includes a five-step process to establish, gather, store, share, and update your personal information. The YTO Guide does not contain instructions on how to obtain legal forms, instead, it will help you discover what documents you may need.

- The **YTO Workbook** is easy to follow and to complete. It will help you to organize your personal records information. The YTO Workbook was created for the use of a general audience; you can skip the sections that do not apply to you. With your completed Workbook, your family or executor can easily step in and facilitate your decisions.

- The **YTO Checklist** will help ensure you have, can locate and access your personal documents and information. The YTO Checklist includes a Quick Pin Checklist, a Quick Password List, an Inventory Quick List Security and a Password Question Check List.

Your True Order is a guide to gathering, organizing and storing your personal records to help you live a better today.

Section I – Your True Order – Guide

The Your True Order (YTO) Guide will help you to identify and gather your essential information. The YTO Guide will take you through a five-step process to establish, gather, store, share, and update your personal information.

Step 1 – Establish

You want to establish yourself, to prove your identity and to share information about who is in your universe. You may want to use the Your True Order Workbook to organize and store the information.

Establish Identity

- Provide your full name, date of birth, address, cell phone number(s), and email address' with associated passwords.

Health

- Provide your medications, list of allergies, vision prescription, and dietary or medical restrictions. Include your blood type and organ donor information.

Personal/Social Media

- Provide your cellular information, all phone numbers, carrier information, account login, passwords and pin numbers.
- Provide each of your personal email accounts, social media accounts, website, domain accounts, login names and passwords.
- Provide your personal computer, and tablet login and passwords.
- Provide your personal storage locations.

Emergency Contact

- Provide name, address, cell phone number(s), and email address. Include the Executor(s) of your Last Will and Testament.

Others Who Depend on You

- Include Family, Children, Parents, Spouse, Significant other.

- Provide full name, date of birth, address, cell phone number(s), and email address for each. Include the name of your nearest relative.
- If applicable, include your child's school information: school name, address, cell phone number(s), and email address, teachers name and class number.

Key Contact

- Provide name, address, cell phone number(s), and email address for each contact. Include Accountant, Dentist, Financial Advisor, Gynecologist, Lawyer, Specialist, Pediatrician, Pharmacist, Physicians, and Veterinarian.

Step 2 – Gather

Step 2 is the longest section to complete. Do not get overwhelmed; simply complete one section at a time — then continue until you complete each section.

To help you organize your personal documents, you may want to invest in a plastic bin, folders or big envelopes as a temporary storage for the items listed below. Use one folder or envelope to store the document listed in each section, allowing you to store like items. If you are gathering, information for a dependent use a separate folder for each person.

Identification

Photo

- Take and print a physical picture of yourself, then of each of your family members (and pets if applicable). On the back of the picture, include full name, height, and date of birth. In case of an emergency, a current picture is the easiest form of identification.

Identification Documents

Gather the original (not photocopies) of the following documents for yourself, and your family. Provided below is a general list of documents; gather the documents that apply to you.

- Birth Certificate, Social Security Card, Health Insurance Card(s)
- Passport, Naturalization Certificate, Permanent Resident Card
- Marriage Certificate/Divorce Certificate
- Any other official, or hard-to-replace documents, i.e. Adoption Papers, Baptismal Certificate
- Copy of your State Identification or Driver's License. A copy because you will need your identification for everyday use ☺

Health Record

- Gather your health records. Include allergy information, dietary restrictions, immunization, medications, vision prescription, donor information. Include your medical insurance provider and all health insurance provider information.

Finances

- Gather your savings and or checking accounts (including physical checks), automated teller machine (ATM) cards, bank cards, and credit cards.

Social Media Information

- Include all social media accounts institution name, login and password. Include Wi-Fi code.

Educational/Training Record

- All relevant paperwork, certificates, scholarship transcripts and awards. Include current copy of resume.

Military Record

- All relevant paperwork. Include military service country, branch, rank, induction date, discharge date, service records, and any medals or citations.

Memberships

- Include Professional, Fraternal, Educational, Religious, Social, Recreational, Charitable, Consumer, Civic, Community, Online groups, Transportation, e.g. airline, train, bus, EZ pass, pay pal, and frequent flyer.

Pet Information

- Provide all relevant paperwork. Include a description of each pet, animal license number and medical records. Include care, food instructions and Guardianship decision.

Directives

Consider Directives as living documents, meaning they are always subject to change depending on your life situation. You must sign and date your directives in the presence of witnesses or a notary public – or both depending on you State law. You must register your Directives in your State's Will/Probate court to be legal.

You can hire legal representation to acquire, complete and register your Directives. If you use legal representation, they may charge you a fee every time you make a change and must reregister the documents in court. You can also go online, download the directive documents, complete the documents and register the directives at your State's Will/Probate Court. You will need to reregister any updated directives with State's Will/Probate court. Each adult requires the documents listed below.

Gather the Original (and a copy) of the following documents:

Advance Health Care Directive

- An advance health care directive is a legal document in which a person specifies what actions to take for their health if they are no longer able to make decisions for himself or herself because of illness or incapacity.

Durable Power of Attorney

- A power of attorney or letter of attorney is a written authorization to represent or act on another's behalf in private affairs, business, or some other legal matter.

Durable Power of Attorney for Finances

- Avoid probate for bank and brokerage accounts complete the 'Pay on Death' designation forms, beneficiary survivor's forms, 'payable-on death' bank accounts (Totten trust) or revocable trust account information.

Funeral Directives

- Provide a Personal Wishes document, Last Words document or Final instructions. Include burial, cremation, and epitaph information.

Guardianship/Care of Children

- A guardian is someone you have named in your last will and living will, as the person who is responsible for your children, if the children are orphaned before reaching the age of 18. Arrange for care of children.

Health Care Proxy

- Medical Power of Attorney include medical letter of instructions. Provide your Do Not Resuscitate Order (DNR), if applicable.

Living Will (Living Revocable Trust)

- A living trust is a tool for determining who will inherit your property when you die. The trust maker (you) creates the living trust while you are alive. To avoid probate, you must register your living will in your State's Will/Probate court to be legal.
- Include Gifts you intend to donate. Giving away property while you are alive may help avoid or reduce probate cost and estate taxes.
- Include all Trusts. A trust is an arrangement under which a person, called a trustee, holds legal title to property for another person.
  - *Charitable Trust* involves making a sizable gift to tax-exempt charity.
  - *Irrevocable Trusts* includes a structured payment for the beneficiary.
  - *Life Insurance Trust* enables policy owner to take the value of life insurance proceeds of out your estate.
  - *Tax-Saving AB Trust* enables spouses to leave their property in trust for their children but give the surviving spouse the right to us it for life.
  - *Qualified Terminable Interest Property* Trust enables the grantor to provide for a surviving spouse, postpone estate taxes, and maintain control of how the trust's assets are distributed once the surviving spouse dies.

Last Will and Testament

- A will or testament is a legal declaration by which a person, names one or more persons (executor(s)) to manage his/her estate and provides for the distribution of his/her property at death. Without a last will and testament, your States Court system will determine what happens to your children, your property, and charge your estate after death.

- Include the disposition of property.

Marital Directives

- Include marital prenuptial and/or postnuptial agreement. Both agreements govern the distribution of a couple's property. A prenuptial agreement is a signed statement of what each partner brought into the union before it occurs, while a postnuptial agreement is created after the union occurs.

Property Directives

- Obtain an original or certified copy of the real estate ownership title documents and estate plan to carry out your intentions with the property. Include Property Title/Deed, *necessary for living trust*, Plat/LOT information, *necessary to determine property line*, and Property Taxes.

- Determine Real Estate Property Ownership:

  - Sole ownership - an individual owns real estate property in his or her name and is generally free to leave property to whom he or she chooses. However, if married or in a registered domestic partnership, the spouse or registered domestic partner may be entitled to a share of the property.

  - Shared ownership - ownership of real estate property is shared with one or more individuals, includes:

    Tenancy in Common – two or more individuals who own a percentage of a real estate property. The owner can leave his or her interest to whomever he or she chooses but again a spouse or registered domestic partner may be entitled to a share of the property.

Joint Tenancy with Right of Survivorship – owners have equal share in real estate property, and when alive an owner can give or sell his or her interest; upon death, the real estate property automatically goes to surviving owners – no matter what the deceased will's or other estate documents state.

Tenancy by Entirety – available to married couples – available in some States only – during life, one owner is not permitted to transfer his or her share of real estate property without consent from the other.

Community Property – any real estate property that spouses earn or acquire during marriage is shared community – meaning each spouse owns half exemption gift or inheritance. At death, each spouse is usually free to leave his or her half of property to any person.

Other Property Directives

Antiques/Art/Intellectual Property

- Obtain an original or certified copy of the Authentication Certificate and Provenances for each work of Art, Antique, and Collectible.
- Include intellectual property rights. Include trademarks, copyright, patents, industrial design rights, and trade secrets. Artistic works include music, literature, logos, discoveries, inventions, words, phrases, symbols, and designs. Include International Standard Book Number (ISBN) ownership information.

Vehicles

- Obtain an original or certified copy of original Title, Registration, Bill of Sale/Receipt, Proof of Insurance and Beneficiary Designation - Transfer on Death Registration forms for each vehicle, e.g. car, truck, boat, skis, snowmobile, utility vehicle, golf cart, motor cycle, scooter, airplane, farming or other heavy equipment, recreational vehicles/trailers.
- Include garage or storage location, mechanic information, alarm system information and spare keys.

Other

- Include information on property you expect to receive.

Insurance

Obtain an original copy of each policy. Provide policy information for yourself, spouse, significant other, parents, and your children. Include the Insurer name, account numbers, policy number, contact number, and addresses. If you conduct business or pay your bills online, include your login name and password, payment amount and payment due date.

Contact each institution and complete Beneficiary/Survivors Designation forms, naming the person or entity that will inherit. Complete, then submit the form and receive acknowledgment of receipt.

Gather the Original (and a copy) of the following documents:

Burial Insurance Policy
- Include Cemetery Plot Deed.

Health Insurance Policy
- Include Medical, Dental, Vision, Prescription.

Homeowners Insurance Policy
- Include Flood Insurance Policy. Include information if policy amount is included in mortgage payment or paid by the mortgage company.

Life Insurance Policy
- Include personal and work life insurance plans.

Long Term Care Insurance Policy
- Include personal and work life insurance plans.

Temporary Disability Policy
- Include personal and work life insurance plans.

Vehicle Insurance Policy
- Include all relevant paperwork for each vehicle.

Other Policy
- Include renter's insurance, appliances, guarantee, and warranty.

Employment

Document and share your employment and or business information.

Employment

- Provide Employer(s) name, address, cell phone number, and email address; Direct supervisor's or 'boss' name, cell phone number, and email address. Provide your title, address, cell phone number, email address, your login name and password. Include paystubs, pay date, pay amount and bank deposit information.

- Include the contact information for the Human Resources and Retirement Department information. Contact the employers Human Resource department and obtain Beneficiary/Survivors Designation forms, naming the person(s) who will inherit your Last Paycheck, Survivors Benefits, 401k Plan, Thrift Savings Plan, Life Insurance Benefit, and Death Benefits. Complete and then submit the forms and ensure you receive acknowledgment of receipt.

- Include pension information.

Self – Employed

- Provide the name, address, cell phone number, and email address for each employer, contract, contractor, and client. Provide business finances include bank accounts, ATM cards, and credit cards. Provide all business income payments i.e., cash, credit, checks. Include receipts, business expenses and liabilities.

Financial/Income

Provide the Business/Institution name, account numbers, policy number, contact number, and addresses for each financial institution. If you conduct business online, include your Login name and password. Contact each institution and complete Beneficiary/Survivors Designation forms or transfer-on death forms.

You can name a beneficiary for each of your retirement accounts, including individual retirement arrangements. If you have vested rights in pension plan, you can name a beneficiary to inherit the pension rights. You can specify how you want the remaining money divided among the beneficiaries.

Finances

Banking Information

- Gather your personal banking information. All saving and checking account information, ATM cards, bank cards, credit cards.
- For each bank account, provide the bank email address/login address, your personal login name, and passwords for each account. Include bank account number, name on the account, type of account, and the bank routing number.
- If you have an ATM and or debit card, include type of card (VISA, Master Card), card Number, card expiration date, the 3-digit CVV Number (Card Verification Value) and your pin number.

Income

- Provide employment income (salary).
- Include Social Security Retirement, Government Pension/Retirement Pension, Inheritance, Annuity, Alimony, Workers Compensation, and or Disability Benefits. Include payment date, payment amount, provide bank deposit information and a current statement.
- Include loans payable and or receivable. Include money owed to you.

Personal Taxes

- Provide a copy of your last three - five years of Personal and Business tax returns.

Credit Reports

- Include a current copy of your credit report for the top three companies Experian, Equifax and TransUnion with your FICO (Fair Isaac Corporation) credit score. Review each report and dispute any discrepancies.

Investment

- Include Government Retirement plan, Thrift Savings Plan, Mutual Funds, Stocks, Individual Retirement Arrangements (IRAs)/Roth IRA including 401 (k) 403 (b) 457 (b), 529 College Savings Plan accounts, CDs (Certificate of Deposit Rates), Stock, Savings Bonds, other Treasury Bonds, Social Security Retirement Estimate and Stock Options.

- Include payment date, payment amount, and bank withdrawal information. Include a current statement.

Business Interest

- Gather information on the stock or stock options you own. Include information if stocks are held by you or by a brokerage company.

- Include amount, broker information. Include a current statement.

Debt/Liability

Credit debts, liens, mortgages and other loans do not disappear upon death. The State will accredit (ascribe, assign) debt to your estate. The items listed below will need to be cancel, paid, and closed.

Provide the company/institution name, account numbers, policy number, contact number, and addresses for each. If you conduct business or pay your bills online, include your Login name and password. Include payment amount and payment due date.

Loans

- Provide current payment information, date of payment and interest rate. Include Bank, Personal, Tuition and Vehicle Loans.

Credit Cards

- Provide Credit Card institution name, email address/login address, your personal login name, and password. Include all credit cards i.e. Department Store Cards, Credit Cards, type of card, (VISA, MasterCard, and or American Express), card number, card expiration date, the 3-digit CVV Number and your pin number. Include annual percentage rate of charge (APR), credit limit, and amount owed.

Property Mortgage/Rental/Lease

- For each property you own, rent, or lease provide current payment, date of payment and interest rate. Include Bank withdrawal information and a current statement. Contact each institution and complete Beneficiary/Survivors Designation forms.

Post Office (PO) Box

- Provide name address of the institution, the box number and address. Include payment amount and payment due date. Obtain an extra key.

Safety Deposit Box

- Provide name address of the institution, the box number and address. Include payment amount and payment due date. Obtain an extra key.

Utility Bills

- Provide information for Gas, Electric, Water, Cable, Home Alarm System, Phone (landline) bill for each property. Internet service provider.
- Include a current statement.

Other Bills /Liens/Collections

- Provide all other bills, e.g. Prime accounts, Storage Units, EZ Pass.
- Include debt collection and any delinquency information e.g., hospital bills, tax lien.

Property

Obtain an original or certified copy of the documents.

Property Information

- Include the address of all your properties i.e., Home, Mobile Homes, Tiny Homes, Vacation Homes, Rentals and Timeshares. Include Property Title/Deed, necessary for living trust, Plat/LOT information, necessary to determine property line, and Property Taxes. Include date of purchase and occupancy dates.

- Include home alarm system, gate or garage codes, and an extra set of keys.

- Include Historical information and documentation if applicable.

- Include property care information, e.g. home repair, maintenance, breaker box locations, septic tanks, water tanks.

Homeowners Owners Association

- Include Homeowners Owners Association name, account numbers, policy number, contact number, and addresses for each institution. If you conduct business or pay your bills online, include your login name, password, and payment amount and payment due date.

Proprietor's Information or Renters Information

- If you are a Proprietor and rent your property, provide the Renter's name, personal information, and phone number. Include lease/rental agreements, payment amount and payment due date. Obtain extra set of keys for other properties.

- If you are a Renter, provide the proprietor's name, address, and phone number. Provide lease/rental agreements. Include payment amount, payment due date, and any money you paid the proprietor, e.g. security payment.

Inventory

Whether you are a homeowner or renter, an accurate household property inventory is a necessity. Create an itemized list of your personal belongings. In case of a loss due to burglary, vandalism, fire or flood, your insurance company will require a list of all items lost or destroyed. Reconstructing a list of belongings from memory is often difficult.

- Take pictures and/or make a video of your belongings. Pictures and videos are the easiest way to show what you have.

Personal Property

- Create an inventory list. Inventory all items in your home. Include all household items – clothes, jewelry, electronics, vehicles, collectibles, and works of art, important receipts, and garage storage. Include a list of loaned jewelry, or coveted belongings.

- Include a description of each item, serial number, purchase date, original cost, and estimated current value. Include authentication of art, antiques, and collectibles with purchase price and projected value.

  If you cannot find original purchase prices of household electronic equipment in your records, check the Internet for the value of electronic gear that is similar in age and features to yours.

Safety Deposit

- Inventory the contents of your safe deposit box at the bank. Obtain an extra key.

Secret Hiding Places/Home Safe

- Inventory the content in your home safe and hiding places. Provide the combination number, passwords or pins and location of the home.

Storage Unit

- Inventory all items in your storage unit. Take pictures and/or make a video of the items you have in storage.

Business Owner

If you only own stock or stock options in a business or businesses skip this section.

Business Ownership

- List full names of Business Owners, including yourself, Job Title or Position. Ownership percentage. Ownership documents.
- What type of business? Do you have partners? What are their rights responsibilities? Provide contact information.

Business Information

- Provide Business Name. Business Start date. If you conduct business online, include your Login name and password.
- Provide main office address, contact number, email address and passwords. Include locations of subsidiaries or branch offices. Include location, access information and keys, combinations, access codes or security cards.
- Provide an original copy of Business documents. Include Business State Registration, Business license, Sales and Tax License, Internal revenue Service Employer ID Number (EIN) tax identification number, Trade Names, Include Domain Registrar and Copyright documentation. Provide Business Website and Server information. Include business insurance coverage. Provide 'Pay on Death' designation forms.

Business Key Individuals

- Provide the name and contact information for business support. Include attorney and accountant.

Business Employees

- Provide the Contact information for Key Employees. Include any employment agreement.

Business Client/Vendor Information

- Provide business Client, Contractor information. Include name, address, cell phone number(s), and email address.
- Provide business Vendor information. Include name, address, cell phone number(s), and email address.
- Include accounting method information, products service maintenance.

Business Finances

- Provide business finances include bank accounts, bank loans/creditors, ATM cards, and credit cards. Include current-year records. Include business income payments i.e., cash, checks.

Business Significant Assets and Liabilities

- Under Assets, include bank and brokerage accounts, insurance, inventory, judgments, real estate, fixtures and equipment, including Point of Sale System, and Credit Card machine. Include vehicles, accounts receivable, copyrights, and trademarks/secrets. Include description, location and provide access information of assets.
- Under Liabilities, provide short and long-term liabilities including significant expenses, (i.e. real estate, equipment rental charges), bank loans, deferred accruals, judgments and retiree benefits worker compensation. Employee benefit programs i.e., retirement, disability, health insurance, workers compensation. Include description, location and provide access information of liabilities.

Business Taxes

- Include a copy of your last three – five years of Business tax returns.

Business - Other

- Document any prior business interest of any legal action in which business has a responsibility or interest that have been resolved and terminated just in case your survivors have questions or face a claim in the future.

Business Ownership Disposition

- Provide Business ownership disposition directions. The options for passing the business to others depends on the form of ownership.

  Generally, if you are alive:

  - *Continue* – the surviving owners will continue to run the business – not an option for sole proprietorship.
  - *Transfer* – the business continues but ownership would be transferred to a specific other.
  - *Sell* – the business will continue to operate but the business itself and your interest would be sold to new owners.
  - *Liquidate* – the business and your interest will dissolve, and any substantial assets will be sold.

  If you are incapacitated or not *alive*:

  - *Sole Proprietorship* – the business will cease – unless the business is inherited by someone who wants to keep the business.
  - *Partnership* – the business can usually continue operate if the remaining partners want to stay in business. A partnership agreement would set the terms of a buy-out.
  - *Limited Liability Company* – the business will dissolve when one-member dies unless, the operating agreement sets out a different plan.
  - *Corporation* – as an independent entity the death of owner has no legal effect on the business. The deceased owner shares are purchased by the corporation, or transferred to an heir. You must determine the terms in the shareholders' agreement.

Step 3 – Store

You have done the work and gathered significant, confidential and personal information. Allow yourself the time you need to organize and store your records. Organized records will alleviate stress since they will be in one place, which will serve as a benefit to you.

You do not have to do it all at once. Set up a schedule to tackle each task. Ask someone you trust to help you if it becomes too overwhelming.

When setting up your organizational system make it is easy to understand so that if anyone needs to find something, he or she will be able to locate your information quickly and easily. The YTO Workbook helps with the organization, storing and sharing of personal information.

Categorize Your Records

- An organizing system can be as simple as a three-ring binder with dividers, folders and/or big envelopes. Clearly label each divider, folder or envelope.
- Organize one section at a time, use one folder or envelope to sort and store the documents listed in the YTO Guide section, allowing you to store like items.
- If you are gathering, information for a dependent use a separate folder for each person.
- Sort your existing records to determine if you should keep them or shred them. Divide documents that fall into a miscellaneous category into general piles like 'To File', 'To Shred' or 'Throw Away'.
    - Check your records for Personally Identifiable Information (PII). After you sort your records, you should check each item for PII, like social security numbers, account numbers, and credit card numbers. Then if you are not going to save the documents, to ensure your safety from identity theft, shred the sensitive records.
- Keeping the most recent records in the front of each folder will help you keep them sorted by date without having to go back and rearrange them.

Find a Place to Store Your Files - And their Backups

- You separated, organized, and categorized your records; you need to find a safe place to store them.

Organizing a Home Filing System

- A system for personal records is a necessity. You need a special place to keep your papers. It could be as simple as a corner of the bedroom, or living room.
- The equipment you will need does not have to be elaborate. Think about a filing cabinet before or a two-drawer cabinet. If you do not have space for a small cabinet, accordion folders, a storage chest that fits under the bed, or a sturdy cardboard boxes of an appropriate size.
- A home computer can be handy, but it is not essential. The essential thing is to know where everything is.

Home Files

- Depending on how often you use a particular file, you may choose to store it in one of three at-home locations: current files, permanent files, or storage files.
  - Current files contain papers that you need frequently. They should be located in a folder in the most accessible drawer in a file cabinet or desk or in the easiest-to-reach boxes. You can also store some of them on a computer hard drive that is backed up consistently to an iCloud account e.g. Bills to pay and paid bills, medical information.
  - Permanent files contain papers that you need less often. Since you do not handle these papers frequently, you can store them in a less accessible file drawer or box or perhaps in a binder or on an external disk drive that you can remove quickly in case of a fire, flood, or other emergency e.g. Education records, Employment records.
  - Storage files are for records that are very rarely used but that may be needed one day e.g. Past income tax records You can store these in a box located in your attic, basement, or closet. Think about discarding files after three years.

Physical Storage

- Decide the physical storage and location of the original documents and copies. Some items you may want to keep on hand for easy access, e.g., driver's license, medical cards or passport.
- You may want to separate the originals and the copies to store them in different locations.

Original

- Keep the original documents in a secured location, preferably fireproof and waterproof safe. You can choose to keep the originals in a safe deposit box or with your legal representative. Obtain extra keys for safety deposit box, and or safe.

Copies

- Keep extra copies of the most important documents in a different location from the originals. For added security, you can keep an electronic copy of your documents as a backup.
- Store the originals documents that you are keeping on hand for easy access, and the copies of your records in a waterproof container, e.g. plastic bin. Then decide where you will keep and store your container i.e., your closet, the garage, the office.
- Create a list or a key to indicate where each important document is located. For example, you might have various locations, and a safety deposit box in which you keep your documents. The YTO Checklist helps to ensure you have all the necessary documents.
- You may want to store your YTO Workbook in a safety deposit box or an attorney, however, doing so will limit access to your workbook. You will have to wait for attorney availability and are limited to bank hours for access. You can choose to keep your YTO Workbook in your secure area, and store your YTO Checklist in an easier to access location.

Electronic Storage

- Paper storage may not be enough. In the case of an emergency, you may not have access to your physical documents. Also, to recover all the documents for yourself and family may be difficult.
- Keeping digital medical records allows you to store and access information easily.
- Converting your documents and files will eliminate paper and free up space in the filing cabinet.
- Scan and then store and save all documents into an external hard drive, as well as, in a secure cloud account.
  - If you do not have a scanner – take a picture with your phone, email the picture to your email account, and store the various emails into one 'Master' folder, then save the file in your external hard drive and onto your secure cloud account.
- Decide the physical storage and location of the external hard drive. Perhaps you have one at home and another in your safety deposit box or with your executor.

Some documents should not be stored in your bank safe-deposit box. It would be difficult to get to them quickly in an emergency. Here are suggestions about where to store some important documents:

<u>Medical Directives</u>

- Give the original copy of all advance medical directives to your health care providers.
- Keep a copy of your advance medical directives, and provide a copy to the person you have chosen to act on your behalf in a medical emergency.

<u>Other Directives</u>

- Give the original copy of each of the directives to your attorney. He or she will store them for you and your loved ones.
- Keep a copy of the documents and provide a copy to others who might be involved later, e.g. Guardianship documents to the legal guardian for your children.

Step 4 – Share

Congratulations, you have done all the work. Share the information.

Share your decisions, you cannot take anything with you, but you can decide what to do with what you acquired. Ensure that someone else knows and understands the family record-keeping system.

Your spouse, adult children, and any others who would need to handle your financial affairs — should know the location of all papers, contracts, documents, policies and other needed information. Each should know to whom to turn for advice in case of emergency.

- You can choose to complete your YTO Workbook to help you assemble personal information, and your YTO Checklist to ensure you have all the necessary documents.
- You can choose to create a centralized document, i.e., a spreadsheet. Print a copy of the centralized document and save the electronic files. Share a paper copy and/or email the electronic version of the centralized document with your executor, attorney or a loved one.
- Share a paper copy of your YTO documents and or email the electronic version of your YTO documents to your executor, attorney or a loved one.
- Share a paper copy of important legal documents directly to the person who is responsible for seeing that your wishes are followed. If you do not want to do that, tell them where you keep the copies.
- Ensure that trusted loved ones or friends know where these documents are, have access, and if necessary a key, or appropriate codes.

Step 5 – Update

To effectively handle and deal with life changes and emergencies requires advance preparation and planning. Well-organized and current records can save time and reduce the stress of finding misplaced documents when you need them in a hurry.

- Consider your personal documents, paperwork as *living* documents. Access to your personal documents is crucial. You may need to add to them, delete, or make changes.
- Changes in life — marriage, a child, a new arrangement, a pet, a move, change in jobs, change in law or military deployment — will require you to update your records, your YTO Workbook and Checklist.
- After you get your records organized, the last step is to keep it free of clutter and, well organized.
- Keep the documents organized and in the right place, be sure to file any new bills or records in your record filing system or in your YTO Workbook and Checklist as soon as possible.
- You can utilize your YTO Workbook and Checklist to store, share, and easily update your information.

Document Your System — And Maintain It

- Records should be reviewed at least once a year to discard items no longer needed. January is a good time for an overhaul, it is the beginning of a new year and it is just before you begin to work on taxes.
- Review, update and back up your files, documents, and workbook regularly; at least every six months, yearly or as needed
- Set up reminders on your calendar, phone and computers.

Conclusion

The Your True Order guide does not cover every life situation. The goal is to help you live a better today by having peace of mind.

You have read the YTO Guide and may feel overwhelmed. The reality is — it is overwhelming — there is a lot to do.

However, you started, and you are working toward your personal success. One way to break down the task is to break them up into smaller, more manageable mini-goals.

- Establish Short-Term Goals, which you complete in less than three months.

  A short-term goal might be to write to an appropriate agency to obtain a copy of an important document.

Then,

- Establish Intermediate Goals, which you complete in three to six months.

  An intermediate goal might be to photograph or videotape your household property or completing Your True Order Workbook.

To stay motivated, visualize the positive outcomes that you will experience when you complete your goal. Evaluate your progress and make changes as needed. Once you achieve a goal, enjoy your accomplishment and give yourself a small reward. Then move on to the next goal.

With motivation, focus, commitment, and discipline, you will achieve your goals and take control of your future.

— Wishing you Peace and Love. O. Escobar

Section II – Your True Order – Workbook

The Your True Order Workbook will help you to record your personal information. The purpose is to organize this information so that you, or others who might have to manage your affairs, can. Well-organized records can save time and reduce the stress of finding misplaced documents when you need them in a hurry. Knowing what you already have can help you decide which important papers you will need to start organizing and/or updating.

The YTO Workbook has a general design to meet the needs of many. You can utilize the Workbook to store, share, and easily update your information. You will need to complete the information requested (if applicable).

About Your – Goals

Short Term Goals

DATE	GOAL

Intermediate Goals

DATE	GOAL

Short Term Goals

DATE	GOAL

Intermediate Goals

DATE	GOAL

Your True Order – Workbook

About Your – Identity

Name (s)	
Alias	
Maiden Name	
Other Names Used	
Date of Birth	
Place of Birth	
Religion	
Address	
Cell Phone *Include Login Pin Number*	
Work Phone	
Home Phone	
Photo Identification	

Health Information

Allergies	
Blood Type	
Dietary Restrictions	
Medications	
Organ Donation	
Vision	
Prescription Renewal Date Dr. Name	

Identification/Certificates

Use the information on your Identification certificates to complete the charts below.

Identification	Information
Birth Certificate	
Social Security Card	
Passport	
Country Passport Expiration Date	
Immunization Records	
Naturalization Papers	
Permanent Residency Card	
Marriage Certificate State & Date	
Divorce Certificate State & Date	
Adoption Papers State & Date	
Driver's License/Identification State & Date	

Religion/Spiritual/Healing	Name of Institution
Baptismal Certificate	
Communion Certificate	
Spiritual Healer	

About Your – Medical/Health Insurance Provider

Medical/Health Insurance Provider

Care Provider	
Membership Number	
ID Number	
Enrollment Code	
Effective Date	
Family Coverage	
Single Coverage	
Address	
Phone	
Email	
City, State, Federal or Private	
Cost of Coverage	
Payment Date	
Co - Pay	
Statements	Paper: ________ Electronic: _________
Policy Information	
Coverage Information includes: Medical Vision Dental Prescription	

Medical/Health Insurance Provider

Care Provider	
Membership Number	
ID Number	
Enrollment Code	
Effective Date	
Family Coverage	
Single Coverage	
Address	
Phone	
Email	
City, State, Federal or Private	
Cost of Coverage	
Payment Date	
Co - Pay	
Statements	Paper: ________ Electronic: _________
Policy Information	
Coverage Information includes; Medical Vision Dental Prescription	

Home Health Care Provider

Health Care Provider Institution Name	
Address	
Phone	
Email	
Cost	
Payment Due Date	
Paid by whom	
Health Care Aid Nurse Name	
Phone	
Email	
Additional Notes	

Nursing Home

Health Care Provider Institution Name	
Address	
Phone	
Email	
Cost	
Payment Due Date	
Paid by whom	
Additional Notes	

About Your – Finances

About Your – Personal Bank Information

Bank Name	
Type of Account	
Title	
Login	
Password	
Account #	
Routing #	
Address	
Phone	
Email	
Pay on Death Form	Date Completed:
Survivors Designation	Date Completed:
Check Book (s)	Yes: __________ No: __________
Statements	Paper: __________ Electronic: __________
ATM Card #	
Type	
CVV	
Expiration Date	
Pin Number	
Additional Notes	

About Your – Personal Bank Information

Bank Name		
Type of Account		
Title		
Login		
Password		
Account #		
Routing #		
Address		
Phone		
Email		
Pay on Death Form	Date Completed:	
Survivors Designation	Date Completed:	
Check Book (s)	Yes: ____________	No: ___________
Statements	Paper: ___________	Electronic: _________
ATM CARD #		
Type		
CVV		
Expiration Date		
Pin Number		
Additional Notes		

About Your – Personal Bank Information

Bank Name		
Type of Account		
Title		
Login		
Password		
Account #		
Routing #		
Address		
Phone		
Email		
Pay on Death Form	Date Completed:	
Survivors Designation	Date Completed:	
Check Book (s)	Yes: ___________	No: ___________
Statements	Paper: ___________	Electronic: __________
ATM CARD #		
Type		
CVV		
Expiration Date		
Pin Number		
Additional Notes		

About Your – Personal Bank Information

Bank Name		
Type of Account		
Title		
Login		
Password		
Account #		
Routing #		
Address		
Phone		
Email		
Pay on Death Form	Date Completed:	
Survivors Designation	Date Completed:	
Check Book (s)	Yes: ___________	No: __________
Statements	Paper: __________	Electronic: _________
ATM CARD #		
Type		
CVV		
Expiration Date		
Pin Number		
Additional Notes		

About Your – Credit Card

Credit Company Name	
Type of Account	
Title	
Login	
Password	
Address	
Phone	
Email	
Survivors Designation	Date Completed:
Statements	Paper: _________ Electronic: _________
Card Number	
Type	
CVV Number	
Expiration Date	
Pin Number	
Credit Limit	
APR Rate	
Amount Owed	
Credit Available	
Account Used to Pay Bill	
Additional Notes	

About Your – Credit Card

Credit Company Name	
Type of Account	
Title	
Login	
Password	
Address	
Phone	
Email	
Survivors Designation	Date Completed:
Statements	Paper: ____________ Electronic: __________
Card Number	
Type	
CVV Number	
Expiration Date	
Pin Number	
Credit Limit	
APR Rate	
Amount Owed	
Credit Available	
Account Used to Pay Bill	
Additional Notes	

About Your – Credit Card

Credit Company Name	
Type of Account	
Title	
Login	
Password	
Address	
Phone	
Email	
Survivors Designation	Date Completed:
Statements	Paper: _________ Electronic: _________
Card Number	
Type	
CVV Number	
Expiration Date	
Pin Number	
Credit Limit	
APR Rate	
Amount Owed	
Credit Available	
Account Used to Pay Bill	
Additional Notes	

About Your – Department Card

Credit Company Name	
Type of Account	
Title	
Login	
Password	
Address	
Phone	
Email	
Survivors Designation	Date Completed:
Statements	Paper: ___________ Electronic: _________
Card Number	
Type	
CVV Number	
Expiration Date	
Pin Number	
Credit Limit	
APR Rate	
Amount Owed	
Credit Available	
Account Used to Pay Bill	
Additional Notes	

About Your – Department Card

Credit Company Name	
Type of Account	
Title	
Login	
Password	
Address	
Phone	
Email	
Survivors Designation	Date Completed:
Statements	Paper: ________ Electronic: _________
Card Number	
Type	
CVV Number	
Expiration Date	
Pin Number	
Credit Limit	
APR Rate	
Amount Owed	
Credit Available	
Account Used to Pay Bill	
Additional Notes	

About Your – Department Card

Credit Company Name	
Type of Account	
Title	
Login	
Password	
Address	
Phone	
Email	
Survivors Designation	Date Completed:
Statements	Paper: ___________ Electronic: _________
Card Number	
Type	
CVV Number	
Expiration Date	
Pin Number	
Credit Limit	
APR Rate	
Amount Owed	
Credit Available	
Account Used to Pay Bill	
Additional Notes	

About Your – Social Media Information

Your Personal Data	Email Address	Password
Personal Email		
Personal Email		
Personal Email		
Work Email		
Facebook		
Instagram		
Twitter		
Skype		
Personal Website		
Domain/IP Information		
Wi-Fi Code		
iCloud Account		

Personal Computer Information

Personal Computer Information	Pin/ Log In	Password
Tablet		
Home Computer		
Laptop		
eBook Reader		
Work Computer		
Anti-Virus		

Educational Information

Educational/Training	Institution
High School	
Degree Achieved	
Date	
Associates' Degree	
Degree Achieved	
Date	
Bachelors' Degree	
Degree Achieved	
Date	
Masters' Degree	
Degree Achieved	
Date	
PHD Degree	
Degree Achieved	
Date	
Certification	
Title	
Date	
Licenses	
License Achieved	
Date	
Scholarship	
Scholarship Amount	
Date	

Personal Resume

Personal Resume	**Year**
Resume(s)	
Work Resume	
Cover Letter	
Recommendations	
Performance Appraisals	
Award Certificates	
Other	

Military

Service Country	
Military Branch	
Dates of Service	
Rank	
Medals	
Citations	
Deployment	

Service Country	
Military Branch	
Dates of Service	
Rank	
Medals	
Citations	

Credit Reports

Institution	FICO Score	Date
Experian		
TransUnion		
Equifax		

Tax Return

Returns & Records	State Filed	Date Filed	Additional Notes
Current – Year			
Prior Year Record			
Prior Year Record			
Prior Year Record			

Storage Locations

Storage Locations	Physical Location
Computers	
External Hard Drives	
Home Safe	
Electronic Files	
Contents of Safe Deposit Box	
Inventory: Pictures/Video	
Personal Property: Pictures/Video	
Safety Deposit Box	
Secret Hiding Locations	
Storage Bins	
Storage Unit	
Other	

Memberships

Organization Name	
Membership Number	
Position Held	
Address	
Email	
Phone	
Fee Tithe Donations	

Organization Name	
Membership Number	
Position Held	
Address	
Email	
Phone	
Fee Tithe Donations	

Organization Name	
Membership Number	
Position Held	
Address	
Email	
Phone	
Fee Tithe Donations	

Memberships

Organization Name	
Membership Number	
Position Held	
Address	
Email	
Phone	
Fee Tithe Donations	

Organization Name	
Membership Number	
Position Held	
Address	
Email	
Phone	
Fee Tithe Donations	

Organization Name	
Membership Number	
Position Held	
Address	
Email	
Phone	
Fee Tithe Donations	

About Your – Advisors

Emergency Contact

Name	
Address	
Cell Phone	
Work Phone	
Home Phone	
Personal Email	

Name	
Address	
Cell Phone	
Work Phone	
Home Phone	
Personal Email	

Executor

Name	
Address	
Cell Phone	
Work Phone	
Home Phone	
Personal Email	
Work Email	

Personal Advisor(s)

Accountant

Name	
Address	
Cell Phone	
Work Phone	
Work Email	
Additional Information	

Dentist

Name	
Address	
Cell Phone	
Work Phone	
Work Email	
Additional Information	

Doctor

Name	
Address	
Cell Phone	
Work Phone	
Work Email	
Additional Information	

Doctor

Name	
Address	
Cell Phone	
Work Phone	
Work Email	
Additional Information	

Financial Advisor

Name	
Address	
Cell Phone	
Work Phone	
Work Email	
Additional Information	

Gynecologist

Name	
Address	
Cell Phone	
Work Phone	
Work Email	
Additional Information	

Healer

Name	
Address	
Cell Phone	
Work Phone	
Work Email	
Additional Information	

Lawyer

Name	
Address	
Cell Phone	
Work Phone	
Work Email	
Additional Information	

Optometrist

Name	
Address	
Cell Phone	
Work Phone	
Work Email	
Additional Information	

Pastor/Priest

Name	
Address	
Cell Phone	
Work Phone	
Work Email	
Additional Information	

Pediatrician

Name	
Address	
Cell Phone	
Work Phone	
Work Email	
Additional Information	

Pharmacist

Name	
Address	
Cell Phone	
Work Phone	
Work Email	
Additional Information	

Physician

Name	
Address	
Cell Phone	
Work Phone	
Work Email	
Additional Information	

Psychiatrist

Name	
Address	
Cell Phone	
Work Phone	
Work Email	
Additional Information	

Specialist

Name	
Address	
Cell Phone	
Work Phone	
Work Email	
Additional Information	

Therapist

Name	
Address	
Cell Phone	
Work Phone	
Work Email	
Additional Information	

Veterinarian

Name	
Address	
Cell Phone	
Work Phone	
Work Email	
Additional Information	

Other

Name	
Address	
Cell Phone	
Work Phone	
Work Email	
Additional Information	

About Your – Family

Spouse – Significant Other

Information	**Relationship: ____________________**
Name	
Other Names	
Date of Birth	
Blood Type	
Social Security Number	
Passport - Naturalization	
Date of Marriage	
Marriage - Divorce Certificate	
Medical Insurance Card(s)	
Driver's License – Identification	
Military Service	
Address	
Cell Phone	
Work Phone	
Home Phone	
Personal Email	
Work Email	
List Names of Children	
Any Directives?	
Any Insurance Policies?	
Additional Notes	

Spouse – Significant Other

Information	**Relationship: ________________________**
Name	
Other Names	
Date of Birth	
Blood Type	
Social Security Number	
Passport - Naturalization	
Date of Marriage	
Marriage - Divorce Certificate	
Medical Insurance Card(s)	
Driver's License – Identification	
Military Service	
Address	
Cell Phone	
Work Phone	
Home Phone	
Personal Email	
Work Email	
List Names of Children	
Any Directives?	
Any Insurance Policies?	
Additional Notes	

Child

Information	**Relationship: ____________________**
Name	
Date of Birth	
Blood Type	
Allergies	
Child Birth Certificate	
Child Social Security Card	
Medical Insurance Card(s)	
Passport/Naturalization	
Driver's License - Identification	
Address	
Cell Phone	
Work Phone	
Home Phone	
Personal Email	
Military Service	
Guardian Name	
School Information	
Contact Info	
Teacher/Class	
Any Directives?	
Any Insurance Policies?	
Miscellaneous	
Other Certificates	

Child

Information	**Relationship: ___________________**
Name	
Date of Birth	
Blood Type	
Allergies	
Child Birth Certificate	
Child Social Security Card	
Medical Insurance Card(s)	
Passport/Naturalization Papers	
Driver's License - Identification	
Address	
Cell Phone	
Work Phone	
Home Phone	
Personal Email	
Military Service	
Guardian Name	
School Information	
Contact Info	
Teacher/Class	
Any Directives?	
Any Insurance Policies?	
Miscellaneous	
Other Certificates	

Parent

Information	**Relationship: ____________________**
Name	
Other Names	
Date of Birth	
Blood Type	
Social Security Number	
Medical Insurance Card(s)	
Date of Marriage	
Date of Divorce	
Military	
List Names of Children	
Address	
Cell Phone	
Work Phone	
Home Phone	
Personal Email	
Work Email	
Any Directives?	
Any Insurance Policies?	
Additional Notes	

Parent

Information	**Relationship:** ______________________
Name	
Other Names	
Date of Birth	
Blood Type	
Social Security Number	
Medical Insurance Card(s)	
Date of Marriage	
Date of Divorce	
Military	
List Names of Children	
Address	
Cell Phone	
Work Phone	
Home Phone	
Personal Email	
Work Email	
Any Directives?	
Any Insurance Policies?	
Additional Notes	

Extended Family

Information	**Relationship: ______________________**
Name	
Date of Birth	
Address	
Cell Phone	
Another Phone	
Personal Email	

Information	**Relationship: ______________________**
Name	
Date of Birth	
Address	
Cell Phone	
Another Phone	
Personal Email	

Information	**Relationship: ______________________**
Name	
Date of Birth	
Address	
Cell Phone	
Another Phone	
Personal Email	

Extended Family

Information	**Relationship:** ______________________
Name	
Date of Birth	
Address	
Cell Phone	
Personal Email	

Information	**Relationship:** ______________________
Name	
Date of Birth	
Address	
Cell Phone	
Personal Email	
Work Email	

Information	**Relationship:** ______________________
Name	
Date of Birth	
Address	
Cell Phone	
Personal Email	
Work Email	

List of Friends

Name	
Address	
Cell Phone	
Email	

Name	
Address	
Cell Phone	
Email	

Name	
Address	
Cell Phone	
Email	

Name	
Address	
Cell Phone	
Email	

Name	
Address	
Cell Phone	
Email	

List of Friends

Name	
Address	
Cell Phone	
Email	

Name	
Address	
Cell Phone	
Email	

Name	
Address	
Cell Phone	
Email	

Name	
Address	
Cell Phone	
Email	

Name	
Address	
Cell Phone	
Email	

About Your – Pets

Pet Name	
Date of Birth	
Breed	
Animal State License	
Medication/Shots	
Allergies/Illness	
Pet Food	
Pet Care	
Pet Guardian	
Additional Information	

Pet Name	
Date of Birth	
Breed	
Animal State License	
Medication/Shots	
Allergies/Illness	
Pet Food	
Pet Care	
Pet Guardian	
Additional Information	

About Your – Directives

Document Name	**Last Will and Testament**
Executor Name	
Address	
Phone	
Email	
Alternate Executor	
State Recorded	Date: ____________
Professional Helper	
Address	
Phone	
Email	
Addendum	

Document Name	**Living Will /Living Revocable Trust**
Executor Name	
Address	
Phone	
Email	
Alternate Executor	
State Recorded	Date: ____________
Professional Helper	
Address	
Phone	
Email	

Document Name	**Medical Directives/ Health Care Proxy**
Executor Name	
Address	
Phone	
Email	
Alternate Executor Name	
State Recorded	Date: ____________
Professional Helper	
Address	
Phone	
Email	

Document Name	**Advance Health Care Directive/DNR**
Executor Name	
Address	
Phone	
Email	
Alternate Executor Name	
State Recorded	Date: ____________
Professional Helper	
Address	
Phone	
Email	

Document Name	**Durable Power of Attorney**
Executor Name	
Address	
Phone	
Email	
Alternate Executor Name	
State Recorded	Date: ____________
Professional Helper	
Address	
Phone	
Email	

Document Name	**Durable Power of Attorney Finances**
Executor Name	
Address	
Phone	
Email	
Alternate Executor Name	
State Recorded	Date: ____________
Professional Helper	
Address	
Phone	
Email	

Document Name	**Guardianship for Children**
Executor Name	
Address	
Phone	
Email	
Alternate Executor Name	
State Recorded	Date: ___________
Professional Helper	
Address	
Phone	
Email	

Document Name	**Property Directives**
Executor Name	
Address	
Phone	
Email	
Alternate Executor Name	
State Recorded	Date: ___________
Professional Helper	
Address	
Phone	
Email	

Document Name	**Marital Agreements**
Executor Name	
Address	
Phone	
Email	
Alternate Executor Name	
State Recorded	Date: ____________
Professional Helper	
Address	
Phone	
Email	

Document Name	**Marital Agreements**
Executor Name	
Address	
Phone	
Email	
Alternate Executor Name	
State Recorded	Date: ____________
Professional Helper	
Address	
Phone	
Email	

Document Name	**Final Instructions/Funeral Instructions**
Executor Name	
Address	
Phone	
Email	
Alternate Executor Name	
State Recorded	Date: ____________
Professional Helper	
Address	
Phone	
Email	

Document Name	**Organ or Body Donation**
I would like to Donate	__ My Body __ Any Needed Organs or Tissues __ Only the following:
Receiving Organization	
Address	
Phone	
Email	
Professional Helper	
Address	
Phone	
Email	

Authentication Certificates

Use the information on your certificates to complete the charts below.

Authentication Certificates	Name of Item	Certificate Number	Date Filed
Copyright Certificate			
Copyright Certificate			
Copyright Certificate			
ISBN			
ISBN			
ISBN			
Authentication Certificate Art			
Art			
Art			
Authentication Certificate Antique			
Antique			
Antique			
Authentication Certificate Collectible			
Collectible			
Collectible			
Authentication Certificate Jewelry			
Jewelry			
Jewelry			

Value List – (Art - Antique – Collectible – Collections)

Item	Date of Purchase	Purchase Price	Estimated Value

About Your – Insurance Policies

Burial Policy

Type of Policy	
Name on Policy	
Owner of Policy	
Policy Number	
Cost	
Designee’	
Burial Organization	
Address	
Email	
Phone Number	
Burial – Plot Location	
Login Online Address	
Login Name	
Password	
Payment Amount	
Payment Due Date	
Payment Account	
Payment Source	
Description of Coverage	
Additional Notes	
Epitaph	

Life Insurance Policy

Type of Policy	
Name on Policy	
Owner of Policy	
Policy Number	
Policy Amount	
Designee'	
Survivor Designation Forms	Date Completed:
Insurance Company	
Address	
Email	
Phone Number	
Login Online Address	
Login Name	
Password	
Payment Amount	
Payment Due Date	
Payment Account	
Payment Source	
Description of Coverage	
Additional Notes	

Life Insurance Policy

Type of Policy	
Name on Policy	
Owner of Policy	
Policy Number	
Policy Amount	
Designee’	
Survivor Designation Forms	Date Completed:
Insurance Company	
Address	
Email	
Phone Number	
Login Online Address	
Login Name	
Password	
Payment Amount	
Payment Due Date	
Payment Account	
Payment Source	
Description of Coverage	
Additional Notes	

Temporary Disability Policy

Type of Policy	
Name on Policy	
Owner of Policy	
Policy Number	
Policy Amount	
Designee’	
Survivor Designation Forms	Date Completed:
Insurance Company	
Address	
Email	
Phone Number	
Login Online Address	
Login Name	
Password	
Payment Amount	
Payment Due Date	
Payment Account	
Payment Source	
Description of Coverage	
Additional Notes	

Long Term Care Insurance Policy

Type of Policy	
Name on Policy	
Owner of Policy	
Policy Number	
Policy Amount	
Designee'	
Survivor Designation Forms	Date Completed:
Insurance Company	
Address	
Email	
Phone Number	
Login Online Address	
Login Name	
Password	
Payment Amount	
Payment Due Date	
Payment Account	
Payment Source	
Description of Coverage	
Additional Notes	

Other Policy

Type of Policy	
Name on Policy	
Owner of Policy	
Policy Number	
Policy Amount	
Designee'	
Survivor Designation Forms	Date Completed:
Insurance Company	
Address	
Email	
Phone Number	
Login Online Address	
Login Name	
Password	
Payment Amount	
Payment Due Date	
Payment Account	
Payment Source	
Description of Coverage	
Additional Notes	

Homeowners Insurance Policy

Type of Policy	
Name on Policy	
Owner of Policy	
Policy Number	
Policy Amount	
Designee'	
Survivor Designation Forms	Date Completed:
Insurance Company	
Address	
Email	
Phone Number	
Login Online Address	
Login Name	
Password	
Payment Amount	
Payment Due Date	
Payment Account	
Payment Source	
Description of Coverage	
Flood Insurance	
Addendums	
Extra Insurance	
Additional Notes	

Homeowners Insurance Policy

Type of Policy	
Name on Policy	
Owner of Policy	
Policy Number	
Policy Amount	
Designee'	
Survivor Designation Forms	Date Completed:
Insurance Company	
Address	
Email	
Phone Number	
Login Online Address	
Login Name	
Password	
Payment Amount	
Payment Due Date	
Payment Account	
Payment Source	
Description of Coverage	
Flood Insurance	
Addendums	
Extra Insurance	
Additional Notes	

Insurance Policies for Others

Burial Policy – Another Person (Spouse, Child, Parent)

Type of Policy	
Name on Policy	
Owner of Policy	
Policy Number	
Cost	
Designee'	
Burial Organization	
Address	
Email	
Phone Number	
Burial – Plot Location	
Login Online Address	
Login Name	
Password	
Payment Amount	
Payment Due Date	
Payment Account	
Payment Source	
Epitaph	
Description of Coverage	
Additional Notes	

Life Insurance Policy – Another Person (Spouse, Child, Parent)

Type of Policy	
Name on Policy	
Owner of Policy	
Policy Number	
Policy Amount	
Designee'	
Survivor Designation Forms	Date Completed:
Insurance Company	
Address	
Email	
Phone Number	
Login Online Address	
Login Name	
Password	
Payment Amount	
Payment Due Date	
Payment Account	
Payment Source	
Description of Coverage	
Additional Notes	

Life Insurance Policy – Another Person (Spouse, Child, Parent)

Type of Policy	
Name on Policy	
Owner of Policy	
Policy Number	
Policy Amount	
Designee'	
Survivor Designation Forms	Date Completed:
Insurance Company	
Address	
Email	
Phone Number	
Login Online Address	
Login Name	
Password	
Payment Amount	
Payment Due Date	
Payment Account	
Payment Source	
Description of Coverage	
Additional Notes	

About Your – Vehicle

Vehicle Type	
Color	
Year	
VIN	
Bill of Sale	Date Bought:
Receipt	Amount Paid:
Title	
Registration	State:
Transfer-On-Death Form	Date Completed:
Type of Insurance Policy	
Name on Policy	
Owner of Policy	
Policy Number	
Policy Amount	
Insurance Company	
Address	
Email	
Phone Number	
Login Name	
Password	
Payment Amount	
Payment Due Date	
Payment Account	
Additional Notes	Garage or Storage Location:

Vehicle

Vehicle Type	
Color	
Year	
VIN	
Bill of Sale	Date Bought:
Receipt	Amount Paid:
Title	
Registration	State:
Transfer-On-Death Form	Date Completed:
Type of Insurance Policy	
Name on Policy	
Owner of Policy	
Policy Number	
Policy Amount	
Insurance Company	
Address	
Email	
Phone Number	
Login Name	
Password	
Payment Amount	
Payment Due Date	
Payment Account	
Additional Notes	Garage or Storage Location:

About Your - Warranty

Item	
Company Name	
Address	
Email	
Phone Number	
Warranty Number	
Start Date	
End Date	
Amount Paid	
Additional Notes	

Item	
Company Name	
Address	
Email	
Phone Number	
Warranty Number	
Start Date	
End Date	
Amount Paid	
Additional Notes	

About Your - Warranty

Item	
Company Name	
Address	
Email	
Phone Number	
Warranty Number	
Start Date	
End Date	
Amount Paid	
Additional Notes	

Item	
Company Name	
Address	
Email	
Phone Number	
Warranty Number	
Start Date	
End Date	
Amount Paid	
Additional Notes	

About Your – Employer Information

Your Title	
Work Number	
Email	
Work Login	
Password	
Employer Name	
Address	
Supervisor Name	
Phone	
Email	
Work Start Date	
Work End Date	
Salary	Net
Pay Date	
Direct Deposit	
Ownership Interest	Yes _______ % No______
Current Benefits	Yes $ _______ No______
Human Resource Department	Phone: Email:
Survivor	Date Completed:
Death Benefit	Date Completed:
Last Paycheck	Date Completed:
Retirement Estimate	Date Completed:
Retirement - Pension	Date Completed:
Thrift Savings 401k Plan	Date Completed:
Work Life Insurance	Date Completed:

Employer Information

Your Title	
Work Number	
Email	
Work Login	
Password	
Employer Name	
Address	
Supervisor Name	
Phone	
Email	
Work Start Date	
Work End Date	
Salary	Net
Pay Date	
Direct Deposit	
Ownership Interest	Yes _______ % No______
Current Benefits	Yes $ _______ No______
Human Resource Department	Phone: Email:
Survivor	Date Completed:
Death Benefit	Date Completed:
Last Paycheck	Date Completed:
Retirement Estimate	Date Completed:
Retirement - Pension	Date Completed:
Thrift Savings 401k Plan	Date Completed:
Work Life Insurance	Date Completed:

About Your – Self Employment

Your Title	
Work Number	
Email	
Additional Notes	

Contractor Employer		
Address		
Phone		
Email		
Work Dates	Start Date:	End Date:
Pay Amount	$ _______	Pay Date:

Contractor Employer		
Address		
Phone		
Email		
Work Dates	Start Date:	End Date:
Pay Amount	$ _______	Pay Date:

Contractor Employer		
Address		
Phone		
Email		
Work Dates	Start Date:	End Date:
Pay Amount	$ _______	Pay Date:

Your – Self-Employment

Contractor Employer Name		
Address		
Phone		
Email		
Work Dates	Start Date:	End Date:
Pay Amount	$ _______	Pay Date:

Contractor Employer Name		
Address		
Phone		
Email		
Work Dates	Start Date:	End Date:
Pay Amount	$ _______	Pay Date:

Contractor Employer Name		
Address		
Phone		
Email		
Work Dates	Start Date:	End Date:
Pay Amount	$ _______	Pay Date:

About Your – Investment Information - Business Interest

About Your – Business Interest

Company Name	
Type of Business	
Email	
Log In	
Pin/Password	
Address	
Phone	
Email	
Ownership Interest	Yes _______ % No______
Stocks/Shares	Yes _______ % Date Bought_______ Amount Paid $______ Current Value $_____
Disposition of Business Interest	Continue_______ Transfer_______ Liquidate_______ Sell__________
Buy - Sell Document	Date Completed:
Do you have physical stock?	Yes _______ No______
Are Stocks with Broker Brokerage Company?	Yes _______ No______
Brokerage Company	
Broker Name	
Address	
Phone	
Email	
Cell Phone	

About Your – Business – Interest

Company Name	
Type of Business	
Email	
Log In	
Pin/Password	
Address	
Phone	
Email	
Ownership Interest	Yes _______ % No______
Stocks/Shares	Yes _______ % Date Bought_______ Amount Paid $______ Current Value $______
Disposition of Business Interest	Continue_______ Transfer_______ Liquidate_______ Sell__________
Buy - Sell Document	Date Completed:
Do you have physical stock?	Yes _______ No______
Are Stocks with Broker Brokerage Company?	Yes _______ No______
Brokerage Company	
Broker Name	
Address	
Phone	
Email	
Cell Phone	
Additional Notes	

About Your – Investment Income/Financial Information

Type of Investment	**Annuity**
Account Number	
Name of Institution	
Address	
Phone	
Email	
Login	
Password	
Survivors Designation	Date Completed:
Contribution Amount	
Contribution Source	
Current Amount	$ _______ Date: _____________

Type of Investment	**Certificate of Deposit (CDs)**
Account Number	
Name of Institution	
Address	
Phone	
Email	
Login	
Password	
Survivors Designation	Date Completed:
Contribution Amount	
Contribution Source	
Current Amount	$ _______ Date: _____________

Investments

Type of Investment	**Federal Pension**
Account Number	
Name of Institution	
Address	
Phone	
Email	
Login	
Password	
Survivors Designation	Date Completed:
Contribution Amount	
Contribution Source	
Current Amount	$ _______ Date: ____________

Type of Investment	**State Pension**
Account Number	
Name of Institution	
Address	
Phone	
Email	
Login	
Password	
Survivors Designation	Date Completed:
Contribution Amount	
Contribution Source	
Current Amount	$ _______ Date: ____________

Investments

Type of Investment	**IRA**
Account Number	
Name of Institution	
Address	
Phone	
Email	
Login	
Password	
Survivors Designation	Date Completed:
Contribution Amount	
Contribution Source	
Current Amount	$ _______ Date: _____________

Type of Investment	**Mutual Fund**
Account Number	
Name of Institution	
Address	
Phone	
Email	
Login	
Password	
Survivors Designation	Date Completed:
Contribution Amount	
Contribution Source	
Current Amount	$ _______ Date: _____________

Investments

Type of Investment	**Roth IRA Account**
Account Number	
Name of Institution	
Address	
Phone	
Email	
Login	
Password	
Survivors Designation	Date Completed:
Contribution Amount	
Contribution Source	
Current Amount	$ _______ Date: ____________

Type of Investment	**Savings Bond**
Account Number	
Name of Institution	
Address	
Phone	
Email	
Login	
Password	
Survivors Designation	Date Completed:
Contribution Amount	
Contribution Source	
Current Amount	$ _______ Date: ____________

Investments

Type of Investment	**Social Security Benefits**
Account Number	
Name of Institution	
Address	
Phone	
Email	
Login	
Password	
Survivors Designation	Date Completed:
Contribution Amount	
Contribution Source	
Current Amount	$ _______ Date: _____________

Type of Investment	**Thrift Savings Plan**
Account Number	
Name of Institution	
Address	
Phone	
Email	
Login	
Password	
Survivors Designation	Date Completed:
Contribution Amount	
Contribution Source	
Current Amount	$ _______ Date: _____________

Investments

Type of Investment	**Treasury Notes**
Account Number	
Name of Institution	
Address	
Phone	
Email	
Login	
Password	
Survivors Designation	Date Completed:
Contribution Amount	
Contribution Source	
Current Amount	$ _______ Date: _____________

Type of Investment	**401(K) Retirement Plan**
Account Number	
Name of Institution	
Address	
Phone	
Email	
Login	
Password	
Survivors Designation	Date Completed:
Contribution Amount	
Contribution Source	
Current Amount	$ _______ Date: _____________

Investments

Type of Investment	**529 College Savings Plan**
Account Number	
Name of Institution	
Address	
Phone	
Email	
Login	
Password	
Survivors Designation	Date Completed:
Contribution Amount	
Contribution Source	
Current Amount	$ _______ Date: _____________

Type of Investment	**Fidelity Investments**
Account Number	
Name of Institution	
Address	
Phone	
Email	
Login	
Password	
Survivors Designation	Date Completed:
Contribution Amount	
Contribution Source	
Current Amount	$ _______ Date: _____________

Investments

Type of Investment Account Number	
Name of Institution	
Address	
Phone	
Email	
Login	
Password	
Survivors Designation	Date Completed:
Contribution Amount	
Contribution Source	
Current Amount	$ _______ Date: _____________

Type of Investment	
Account Number	
Name of Institution	
Address	
Phone	
Email	
Login	
Password	
Survivors Designation	Date Completed:
Contribution Amount	
Contribution Source	
Current Amount	$ _______ Date: _____________

About Your – Income/Financial Information

Type of Benefit	**Alimony**
Account Number	
Name of Institution	
Address	
Phone	
Email	
Login	
Password	
Survivors Designation	Date Completed:
Pay Amount	
Pay Date	
Deposit Information	

Type of Benefit	**Disability Benefits**
Account Number	
Name of Institution	
Address	
Phone	
Email	
Login	
Password	
Survivors Designation	Date Completed:
Pay Amount	
Pay Date	
Deposit Information	

Finances

Type of Benefit	**Inheritance**
Account Number	
Name of Institution	
Address	
Phone	
Email	
Login	
Password	
Survivors Designation	Date Completed:
Pay Amount	
Pay Date	
Deposit Information	

Type of Benefit	**Social Security Benefits**
Account Number	
Name of Institution	
Address	
Phone	
Email	
Login	
Password	
Survivors Designation	Date Completed:
Pay Amount	
Pay Date	
Deposit Information	

Finances

Type of Benefit	**Stock/Bonds**
Account Number	
Name of Institution	
Address	
Phone	
Email	
Login	
Password	
Survivors Designation	Date Completed:
Pay Amount	
Pay Date	
Deposit Information	

Type of Benefit	**Retirement Benefits**
Account Number	
Name of Institution	
Address	
Phone	
Email	
Login	
Password	
Survivors Designation	Date Completed:
Pay Amount	
Pay Date	
Deposit Information	

Finances

Type of Benefit	**Investment Plan**
Account Number	
Name of Institution	
Address	
Phone	
Email	
Login	
Password	
Survivors Designation	Date Completed:
Pay Amount	
Pay Date	
Deposit Information	

Type of Benefit	**Workers Compensation**
Account Number	
Name of Institution	
Address	
Phone	
Email	
Login	
Password	
Survivors Designation	Date Completed:
Pay Amount	
Pay Date	
Deposit Information	

Finances

Type of Benefit	**Lottery**
Account Number	
Name of Institution	
Address	
Phone	
Email	
Login	
Password	
Survivors Designation	Date Completed:
Pay Amount	
Pay Date	
Deposit Information	

Type of Benefit	**Other**
Account Number	
Name of Institution	
Address	
Phone	
Email	
Login	
Password	
Survivors Designation	Date Completed:
Pay Amount	
Pay Date	
Deposit Information	

About Your – Liability – Other Debt Information

Type of Loan	**Tuition**
Lender Name	
Account Number	
Address	
Phone	
Email	
Amount Borrowed	
Amount Owed	
Interest Rate	
Payment Date	
Payment Amount	
Account to Pay Loan	

Type of Loan	**Bank Loan**
Account Number	
Lender Name	
Address	
Phone	
Email	
Amount Borrowed	
Amount Owed	
Interest Rate	
Payment Date	
Payment Amount	
Account to Pay Loan	

Debt

Type of Loan	**Personal Loan**
Account Number	
Lender Name	
Address	
Phone	
Email	
Amount Borrowed	
Amount Owed	
Interest Rate	
Payment Date	
Payment Amount	
Account to Pay Loan	

Type of Loan	**Hospital Bill**
Account Number	
Lender Name	
Address	
Phone	
Email	
Amount Borrowed	
Amount Owed	
Interest Rate	
Payment Date	
Payment Amount	
Account to Pay Loan	

Debt

Type of Loan	**Collection**
Account Number	
Lender Name	
Address	
Phone	
Email	
Amount Borrowed	
Amount Owed	
Interest Rate	
Payment Date	
Payment Amount	
Account to Pay Loan	

Type of Loan	**Other**
Account Number	
Lender Name	
Address	
Phone	
Email	
Amount Borrowed	
Amount Owed	
Interest Rate	
Payment Date	
Payment Amount	
Account to Pay Loan	

Other

Type	**Cellular Information**
Account Number	
Institution Name	
Address	
Phone	
Email	
Login	
Password	
Pin Number	
Payment Amount	
Renewal Date	
Amount Owed	
Renewal Date	

Type	**Post Office Box**
Account Number	
Location	
Institution Name	
Address	
Phone	
Email	
Login	
Password	
Payment Amount	
Renewal Date	

Other

Type	**Safety Deposit Box**
Account Number	
Location	
Institution Name	
Address	
Phone	
Email	
Login	
Password	
Payment Amount	
Renewal Date	
Additional Notes	

Type	**Storage Unit**
Account Number	
Location	
Institution Name	
Address	
Phone	
Email	
Login	
Password	
Payment Amount	
Renewal Date	
Additional Notes	

About Your – Property Information

Property – Information

Property Address	
Owner Name (s)	
Address	
Phone	
Property Title/Deed Name(s)	
Title/Deed #	
State	
Plat/LOT Information	
Property Taxes	
School Zone	
Historical Information	
Historical Documentation	
Homeowners Owners Association	
Address	
Phone	
Email	
Home Repairs	
Home Information	
Additional Notes Home Alarm System Gate or Garage Codes Extra Set of Keys	

Mortgage – Payment Information

Mortgage Company Name	
Title of Account	
Account Owner	
Account Number	
Login	
Password	
Address	
Phone	
Email	
Survivors Designation	Date Completed:
Statements	Paper: __________ Electronic: _________
Type of Mortgage	
Total Mortgage Amount	
Years of Mortgage	
APR Rate	
Payment Date	
Mortgage Payment	
Includes Taxes?	Yes: ____ No: _____ Amount: ________
Includes PMI?	Yes: ____ No: _____ Amount: ________
Include Homeowners Insurance Payment	Yes: ____ No: _____ Amount: ________
Revolving Credit Limit?	Yes: ____ No: _____ Amount: ________
Additional Notes	

About You – Renters/Proprietor Information

Renter Information

Property Address	
Proprietor Name	
Phone	
Email	
Renter Name	
Email	
Phone Number	
Work Number	
Renter Credit Report	Date Completed:
Renter Employer Information	
Lease Agreement	
Start Date	
End Date	
Amount of Rent	
Security Deposit	
Escrow Amount	
Rent Due Date	Yes: ____ No: _____ Amount: ________
Utilities Included	Yes: ____ No: _____
List Utilities Not Included	
Name on Utilities Not Included w/Rent	
Additional Notes	

Property – Utility Information

Type	**Home Alarm**
Name on Account	
Alarm Code	
Account Number	
Institution Name	
Address	
Phone	
Email	
Login	
Password	
Payment Amount	
Payment Date	

Type	**Cable**
Name on Account	
Wi-Fi Code	
Account Number	
Institution Name	
Address	
Phone	
Email	
Login	
Password	
Payment Amount	
Payment Date	

Property – Utility Information

Type	**Electric**
Name on Account	
Account Number	
Institution Name	
Address	
Phone	
Email	
Login	
Password	
Payment Amount	
Payment Date	
Payment Plan	

Type	**Gas**
Name on Account	
Account Number	
Institution Name	
Address	
Phone	
Email	
Login	
Password	
Payment Amount	
Payment Date	
Payment Plan	

Property – Utility Information

Type	**Phone (Landline)**
Name on Account	
Account Number	
Institution Name	
Address	
Phone	
Email	
Login	
Password	
Payment Amount	
Payment Date	

Type	**Water**
Name on Account	
Account Number	
Institution Name	
Address	
Phone	
Email	
Login	
Password	
Payment Amount	
Payment Date	

Property – Utility Information

Type	**Landscaping Company**
Name on Account	
Account Number	
Institution Name	
Address	
Phone	
Email	
Login	
Password	
Payment Amount	
Payment Date	

Type	
Name on Account	
Account Number	
Institution Name	
Address	
Phone	
Email	
Login	
Password	
Payment Amount	
Payment Date	

About Your – Business Owner

Business Name		
Business Start Date		
Type of Business		
Business Address		
Phone		
Email		
Other Locations		
Phone		
Your Title		
Work Number		
Work Email		
Password		
Corporation	Start Date:	End Date:
Limited Liability Company	Start Date:	End Date:
Partnership	Start Date:	End Date:
Sole Proprietorship	Start Date:	End Date:
Ownership Interest	Yes _______ %	No______
Stocks/Shares	Yes _______ % Amount Paid $_______	Date Bought_______ Current Value $______
Disposition of Business	Continue_______ Liquidate_______	Transfer_______ Sell__________
Disposition of Business Interest	Continue_______ Liquidate_______	Transfer_______ Sell__________
Buy - Sell Document	Date Completed:	
Additional Notes		

About Your – Business – Key Individuals

Business Name	
Attorney Name	
Address	
Phone	
Email	

Business Name	
Accountant Name	
Address	
Phone	
Email	

Business Name	
Address	
Phone	
Email	

Business Name	
Address	
Phone	
Email	

About Your – Business – List Owners – Partners or Officers

Business Name		
Name		
Title		
Address		
Phone		
Email		
Ownership Interest	Yes _______ %	No______

Business Name		
Name		
Title		
Address		
Phone		
Email		
Ownership Interest	Yes _______ %	No______

Business Name		
Name		
Title		
Address		
Phone		
Email		
Ownership Interest	Yes _______ %	No______

About Your – Business – List Owners – Partners or Officers

Business Name	
Name	
Title	
Address	
Phone	
Email	
Ownership Interest	Yes _______ % No______

Business Name	
Name	
Title	
Address	
Phone	
Email	
Ownership Interest	Yes _______ % No______

Business Name	
Name	
Title	
Address	
Phone	
Email	
Ownership Interest	Yes _______ % No______

About Your – Business – Income

Business Name	
Salary	Net:
Pay Date	
Direct Deposit	

About Your – Business – Pension

Business Name	
401k Plan Designation	Date Completed:
Death Benefit Designation	Date Completed:
Last Paycheck Designation	Date Completed:
Life Insurance Designation	Date Completed:
Pension/Designation Form	Date Completed:
Survivor Designation Forms	Date Completed:
Workers Compensation	Date Completed:

About Your – Business – Information

Business Name	

State - Small Business Account	
Email	
Log in	
Password	

Business License #	
State Filed	Date: __________
Additional Notes	

Business Ownership Papers	
State Filed	Date: __________
Additional Notes	

Employer ID Number (EIN)	
State Filed	Date: __________
Additional Notes	

Sales/Tax License	
State Filed	Date: __________
Additional Notes	

State Registration	
State Filed	Date: __________
Additional Notes	

About Your – Business – Information

State Tax ID	
State Filed	Date: __________
Additional Notes	

Trade Name	
State Filed	Date: _________
Additional Notes	

Trademark/Logo	
State Filed	Date: __________
Additional Notes	

Copy Right	
State Filed	Date: __________
Additional Notes	

Cellular Information	Phone Number: __________________
Account Number	
Institution Name	
Phone	
Email	
Login	
Password	
Pin Number	
Payment Amount	
Renewal Date	
Amount Owed	

About Your – Business – Insurance

Type of Policy	
Name on Policy	
Owner of Policy	
Policy Number	
Policy Amount	
Designee’	
Survivor Designation Forms	Date Completed:
Insurance Company	
Address	
Email	
Phone Number	
Login Online Address	
Login Name	
Password	
Payment Amount	
Payment Due Date	
Payment Account	
Payment Source	Check: Automatic Withdrawal:
Description of Coverage	
Additional Notes	

About Your – Business – Media Information

Business Name	

Business Web Site	

Business IP Server	

Business Web Page Server	
Address	
Phone	
Email	
Login	
Password	
Payment Amount	
Payment Due Date	
Payment Account	
Payment Source	

Domain Registrar	
Address	
Phone	
Email	
Login	
Password	

About Your – Business – Media Information

Domain Name	
Purchase Date	
Renewal date	
Amount	
Payment Source	

Domain Name	
Purchase Date	
Renewal date	
Amount	
Payment Source	

Domain Name	
Purchase Date	
Renewal date	
Amount	
Payment Source	

Domain Name	
Purchase Date	
Renewal date	
Amount	
Payment Source	

Domain Name	
Purchase Date	
Renewal date	

About Your – Business – Media Information

Business Email Account	
Login	
Password	

Facebook	
Login	
Password	

Instagram	
Login	
Password	

Login	
Password	

Login	
Password	

Login	
Password	

Login	
Password	

About Your – Business – Hardware Information

Computer	
Login	
Password	

Laptop	
Login	
Password	

Tablet	
Login	
Password	

Security System	
Login	
Password	

Safety Deposit	
Login	
Password	

Office Safe	
Login	
Password	

Login	
Password	

About Your – Business – Software Information

Accounting Program	
Login	
Password	

Software Account	
Login	
Password	

Pay Pal	
Login	
Password	

Login	
Password	

Login	
Password	

One Drive Account	
Login	
Password	
Purchase Date	
Renewal Date	
Amount	
Payment Source	

About Your – Business – Software Information

Anti -Virus	
Account #	
Login	
Password	
Purchase Date	
Renewal Date	
Amount	
Payment Source	

Credit Card Machine	
Account #	
Login	
Password	
Purchase Date	
Renewal Date	
Amount	
Payment Source	

Point of Sale System	
Account #	
Login	
Password	
Purchase Date	
Renewal Date	
Amount	
Payment Source	

About Your – Business – Key Client Information

Business Name	
Client Name	
Address	
Phone	
Email	
Additional Notes	

Business Name	
Client Name	
Address	
Phone	
Email	
Additional Notes	

Business Name	
Client Name	
Address	
Phone	
Email	
Additional Notes	

About Your – Business – Key Contractor Information

Business Name	
Name	
Type of Work	
Address	
Phone	
Email	
Additional Notes	

Business Name	
Name	
Type of Work	
Address	
Phone	
Email	
Additional Notes	

Business Name	
Name	
Type of Work	
Address	
Phone	
Email	
Additional Notes	

About Your – Business – Key Employee Information

Business Name	
Name	
Title/Position	
Address	
Phone	
Email	
Additional Notes	

Business Name	
Name	
Title/Position	
Address	
Phone	
Email	
Additional Notes	

Business Name	
Name	
Title/Position	
Address	
Phone	
Email	
Additional Notes	

About Your – Business – Bank Information

Business Name	
Bank Name	
Type of Account	
Title	
Login	
Password	
Account #	
Routing #	
Address	
Phone	
Email	
Pay on Death Form	Date Completed:
Survivors Designation	Date Completed:
Statements	Paper: ___________ Electronic: _________
ATM Card	
Type	
CVV	
Expiration Date	
Pin Number	
Additional Notes	

About Your – Business – Bank Information

Business Name	
Bank Name	
Type of Account	
Title	
Login	
Password	
Account #	
Routing #	
Address	
Phone	
Email	
Pay on Death Form	Date Completed:
Survivors Designation	Date Completed:
Statements	Paper: ____________ Electronic: __________
ATM Card	
Type	
CVV	
Expiration Date	
Pin Number	
Additional Notes	

About Your – Business – Credit Card

Business Name	
Credit Company Name	
Type of Account	
Title	
Login	
Password	
Address	
Phone	
Email	
Survivors Designation	Date Completed:
Statements	Paper: ___________ Electronic: _________
Card Number	
Type	
CVV Number	
Expiration Date	
Pin Number	
Credit Limit	
APR Rate	
Amount Owed	
Credit Available	
Account Used to Pay Bill	
Additional Notes	

About Your – Business – Credit Card

Business Name	
Credit Company Name	
Type of Account	
Title	
Login	
Password	
Address	
Phone	
Email	
Survivors Designation	Date Completed:
Statements	Paper: ____________ Electronic: __________
Card Number	
Type	
CVV Number	
Expiration Date	
Pin Number	
Credit Limit	
APR Rate	
Amount Owed	
Credit Available	
Account Used to Pay Bill	
Additional Notes	

About Your – Business – Loan

Business Name	
Type of Loan	
Lender Name	
Address	
Phone	
Email	
Amount Borrowed	
Amount Owed	
Interest Rate	
Payment Date	
Payment Amount	
Account to Pay Loan	

Business Name	
Type of Loan	
Lender Name	
Address	
Phone	
Email	
Amount Borrowed	
Amount Owed	
Interest Rate	
Payment Date	
Payment Amount	
Account to Pay Loan	

About Your – Business – Taxes

Returns & Records	State Filed	Date Filed	Additional Notes
Current – Year			
Prior Year Record			
Prior Year Record			
Prior Year Record			
Prior Year Record			

About Your – Business – Liability

Business Name	
Accounts Payable	
Taxes	
Wages	
Accrued Expenses	
Deferred Revenues	
Debts	
Other	

About Your – Business – Assets

Business Name	
Inventory (Merchandise, Raw Materials, Finished and Unfinished Products not yet been sold)	
Common Stock	
Preferred Stock	
Retained Earnings	
Current Assets (Cash, Other Liquid Items)	
Long-Term Assets (Real Estate, Equipment)	
Prepaid and Deferred Assets (Insurance, Rent, Interest)	
Intangible Assets (Trademarks, Patents, ISBN, Copyrights, Goodwill)	
Other	

Personal Notes

Section III – Your True Order – Checklist

For peace of mind, in knowing that if anything happens to you, you — and your family will be prepared. The Your True Order Checklist helps you ensure that you have gathered and organized all your important documents. The YTO Checklist is a convenient reference to locate and access all your critical documents. It includes a Quick Pin Checklist, a Quick Password List, an Inventory Quick List Security and a Password Question Check List. As a bonus, included is a Quick Net Worth Statement as a means of keeping tabs on your financial progress.

What is the primary locations of your important documents?

- It is important to gather and organize your personal documents and decide where to store the documents and annotate the location of the documents. Consider consolidating storage locations, for ease of access and simplicity.

Location Key

- Create a "key" to indicate where each important document is located. For example, you might have various locations, and a safety deposit box in which you keep your documents and records. In which case, your "key" might resemble the example below.

EXAMPLE

KEY	LOCATION
1	Attorney
2	Bank Safety Deposit Box
3	Carry with You Always
4	Computer/Laptop/External Hard Drive
5	Executor
6	Home File Cabinet (preferably fireproof)
7	iCloud/ External Hard Drive
8	Portable Fireproof Box
9	Primary Doctor
10	Relative/Friend
11	Other

Complete the Key Location Chart Below

About Your – Key Location

KEY	LOCATION

Your True Order – Checklist

About Your – Checklist

About Your – Your True Order

Got It	Your True Order	Location	
		Original	Copy
√	*Example*	*1 & 5*	*4 & 10*
	Your True Order Work Book		
	Your True Order Checklist		

About Your – Storage Locations

Got It	Your – Storage Locations	Location
	Computers	
	External Hard Drive	
	Home Safe/Portable Fireproof Safe	
	Safety Deposit Box	
	Secret Hiding Location	
	Storage Unit	

About Your – Identity

Got It	Your – Identity	Location	
		Original	Copy
	Photo		
	Photo Identification		
	Driver's License		
	State Identification		
	Passport		

About Your – Identity

Got It	Your – Identification	Location	
		Original	Copy
	Birth Certificate		
	Social Security Card		
	Naturalization Papers		
	Permanent Residency Card		
	Marriage/Divorce Certificate		
	Adoption Papers		
	Driver's License		
	Employment Identification		

About Your – Finances – Personal Bank Information

Got It	Your – Identity	Location	
		Original	Copy
	Bank – Checks		
	Bank – Savings Account		
	ATM Cards		
	Pay on Death Form		
	Survivors Designation		

About Your – Finances – Credit Information

Got It	Your – Credit Information	Location	
		Original	Copy
	Credit Cards		
	Department Cards		

About Your – Health Information

Got It	Your – Health Provider	Location	
		Original	Copy
	Medical Insurance Provider		
	Health Insurance Provider		
	Home Health Care		

Got It	Your – Health Records	Location	
		Original	Copy
	Allergy Records		
	Blood Type		
	Dietary Restrictions		
	Immunization Records		
	Medical/Surgical Treatments		
	Medications		
	Organ Donor Information		
	Vision		
	Prescription		

About Your – Religion/Spiritual/Healing

Got It	Your – Religion Spiritual Healing	Location	
		Original	Copy
	Baptismal Certificate		
	Communion Certificate		

About Your – Social Media Information

Got It	Your – Social Media	Location	
		Original	Copy
	Personal Email		
	Work Email		
	Facebook		
	Instagram		
	Twitter		
	Personal Website		
	Domain/IP Information		

About Your – Personal Computer Information

Got It	Your – Personal Computer	Location	
		Original	Copy
	Tablet		
	Home Computer		
	Laptop		
	eBook Reader		
	Work Computer		
	Anti-Virus		
	One Drive Account		
	Microsoft Account		

About Your – Educational Information

Got It	Your – Education	Location	
		Original	Copy
	High School		
	Associates' Degree		
	Bachelors' Degree		
	Masters' Degree		
	PHD Degree		
	Certification		
	Licenses		
	Scholarship		

About Your – Education

Got It	Your – Resume	Location	
		Original	Copy
	Resume		
	Work Resume		
	Cover Letter		
	Letters of Recommendation		
	Performance Appraisals		
	Award Certificates		

About Your – Military

Got It	Your – Military	Location	
		Original	Copy
	Service Record		
	Medal		

About Your – Credit Report

Got It	Your – Credit Report	Location	
		Original	Copy
	Experian		
	TransUnion		
	Equifax		
	FICO Score		

About Your – Tax Return

Got It	Your – Tax Return	Location	
		Original	Copy
	Current – Year		
	Prior Year Record		
	Property Tax		

About Your – Inventory

Got It	Your – Inventory List	Location	
		Original	Copy
	Inventory of Home Safe		
	Inventory of Personal Property		
	Inventory of Safety Deposit Box		
	Inventory of Storage Unit		
	Inventory Pictures/Video/List		

About Your – Memberships

Got It	Your – Memberships	Location	
		Original	Copy
	Charitable		
	Educational		
	Fraternal		
	Professional		
	Religious		
	Social		
	Transportation		

About Your – Advisors

Got It	Your – Advisors	Location	
		Original	Copy
	Executor		
	Accountant		
	Dentist		
	Doctor		
	Financial Advisor		
	Gynecologist		
	Lawyer		
	Optometrist		
	Pastor/Priest		
	Pediatrician		
	Personal Advisor		
	Physician		
	Veterinarian		

About Your – Spouse - Significant Other

Got It	Your – Spouse Significant	Location	
		Original	Copy
	Identity Information		
	Medical Information		
	Marriage – Divorce Information		
	Military Information		
	Children Information		
	Directives		
	Insurance Policies		

About Your – Child

Got It	Your – Child	Location	
		Original	Copy
	Identity Information		
	Medical Information		
	Guardian Information		
	Military Information		
	School Information		
	Directives		
	Insurance Policies		

About Your – Parent

Got It	Your – Parent	Location	
		Original	Copy
	Identity Information		
	Medical Information		
	Guardian Information		
	Military Information		
	Directives		
	Insurance Policies		

About Your –Family/Friends

Got It	Your – Family/Friends	Location	
		Original	Copy
	Your – Extended Family		
	Your – List of Friends		

About Your – Pet Information

Got It	Your – Pet Information	Location	
		Original	Copy
	Pet Information		

About Your – Directives

Got It	Your – Directives	Location	
		Original	Copy
	Advance Health Care Directive		
	Do Not Resuscitate		
	Power of Attorney		
	Power of Attorney for Finances		
	Funeral Directives		
	Final Instruction		
	Guardianship/Care of Children		
	Medical Directives		
	Living Will		
	Last Will and Testament		
	Marital Directives		
	Property Directives		
	Organ Donation		

About Your – Other Directives

Got It	Your – Other Directives	Location	
		Original	Copy
	Antique		
	Art		
	Authentication Certification		
	Collectibles		
	Collections		
	Intellectual Property		
	Jewelry		

About Your – Vehicles

Got It	Your – Vehicles	Location	
		Original	Copy
	Vehicle		
	Vehicle		
	Garage		
	Spare Keys		

About Your – Warranty

Got It	Your – Warranty	Location	
		Original	Copy

About Your – Insurance Policies

Got It	Your – Insurance Policies	Location	
		Original	Copy
	Burial Policy		
	Life Insurance Policy		
	Temporary Disability Policy		
	Long Term Care Insurance Policy		
	Other Policy		
	Homeowners Insurance Policy		
	Flood Insurance		
	Apartment Insurance		
	Vehicle Insurance		
	Personal Property Insurance Jewelry, Antique, Art		

About Your – Insurance Policies – For Others

Got It	Your – Insurance Policy for Others	Location	
		Original	Copy
	Burial Policy – Spouse		
	Burial Policy – Child		
	Burial Policy – Parent		
	Burial Policy – Other		
	Life Insurance Policy – Spouse		
	Life Insurance Policy – Child		
	Life Insurance Policy – Parent		
	Life Insurance Policy – Other		

About Your – Current Employer Information

Got It	Your – Current Employer Information	Location	
		Original	Copy
	Employee Information		
	Employer Information		
	Salary		
	Current Benefits		
	Life Insurance		
	Ownership Interest		
	Retirement – Pension -401K Plan		
	Survivors Designation		

About Your – Previous Employer Information

Got It	Your – Previous Employer Information	Location	
		Original	Copy
	Employer Information		
	Benefits – Insurance – Pension		
	Survivors Designation		

About Your

Got It	Your – Inventory List	Location	
		Original	Copy
	Business Information		
	Contractor Information		
	Client Information		
	Income		
	Expenses		

About Your – Business Interest

Got It	Your – Business Interest	Location	
		Original	Copy
	Company Name		
	Ownership Interest		
	Stocks/Shares		
	Disposition of Business Interest		
	Survivors Designation		

About Your – Investment

Got It	Your – Investment	Location	
		Original	Copy
	Annuity		
	CD		
	Federal Pension		
	State Pension		
	IRA		
	Mutual Fund		
	Roth IRA Account		
	Savings Bond		
	Social Security Benefits		
	Thrift Savings Plan		
	Treasury Notes		
	401(K) Retirement Plan		
	529 College Savings Plan		

About Your – Income/Financial Information

Got It	Your – Income/Financial Information	Location	
		Original	Copy
	Alimony		
	Disability Benefits		
	Inheritance		
	Social Security Benefits		
	Stock/Bonds		
	Retirement Benefits		
	Investment Plan		
	Workers Compensation		
	Lottery		

About Your – Liability - Other Debt Information

Got It	Your – Debt/Liability	Location	
		Original	Copy
	Bank Loan		
	Collection		
	Hospital Bill		
	Lien(s)		
	Personal Loan		
	Safety Deposit Box		
	Storage Unit		
	Tuition		

About Your – Property Information

Got It	Your – Your – Property Information	Location	
		Original	Copy
	Property Title/Deed		
	Plat/LOT Information		
	Property Taxes		
	School Zone		
	Homeowners Owners Association		
	Mortgage Payment Information		
	Historical Documents		
	Cable		
	Electric		
	Gas		
	Home Alarm System		
	Phone (Landline)		
	Water		
	Spare Keys		

About Your – Renters/Proprietor Information

Got It	Your – Your – Renters/Proprietor	Location	
		Original	Copy
	Lease		
	Proprietor Information		
	Renter Information		
	Escrow Information		
	Spare Keys		

About Your – Business (Owner)

Got It	Your – Business (Owner)	Location	
		Original	Copy
	Business Information		
	Type of Business		
	Business License #		
	Business Ownership Papers		
	Employer ID Number (EIN)		
	State Sales/Tax License		
	Tax ID		
	Trade Name		
	Copy Right		
	Logo		
	Ownership Interest		
	Stocks/Shares		
	Disposition of Business		
	Disposition of Business Interest		
	Buy - Sell Document		
	Survivor Designation Forms		
	Key Business Owners – Partners – Officers		
	Key Individual(s)		
	Key Client		
	Key Contractor		
	Key Employee		
	Business Lease		
	Spare Keys		

About Your – Business

Got It	Your – Business	Location	
		Original	Copy
	Business – Insurance		
	Business – Pension		
	Workers Compensation		
	Employee Salary		
	Employee Benefits		

Got It	Your – Business Media Information	Location	
		Original	Copy
	Business IP Server		
	Business Web Page Server		
	Domain Name & Registrar		
	Business Email Account		
	Hardware Information		
	Software Information		

Got It	Your – Business Finances	Location	
		Original	Copy
	Bank Information		
	Credit Card		
	Loan		
	Business Taxes		
	Inventory		
	Liability		
	Assets		

About Your – Quick Pin List

Bank Name	Type	Type	Card Number	Date	CVV	Pin
Bank	Visa MC AMEX	Debit Credit	0000 0000 0000 0000	010/0000	000	0000

About Your – Quick Pin List

Bank Name	Type	Type	Card Number	Date	CVV	Pin

About Your – Quick Password List

Institution Name	Email Address	Password

About Your – Quick Password List

Institution Name	Email Address	Password

About Your – Security Password Question Check List

Question	Answer
What city where you born in?	
What is the first and last name of your first boyfriend or girlfriend?	
What is the name of the road you grew up on?	
What is the name of your favorite pet?	
What Is your favorite book?	
What is your favorite color?	
What is your favorite food?	
What is your mother's maiden name?	
What was the first company that you worked for?	
What was your favorite place to visit as a child?	
Where did you go to high school/college?	
Where did you meet your spouse?	
Where is your favorite place to vacation?	
Who is your favorite actor, musician, or artist?	

About Your – Inventory Quick List

Category	Item	Purchase Date	Purchase Price
Clothing			
Computer Equipment			
Kitchen Appliances			
Entertainment Equipment			
Exercise Equipment			
Furniture			
Health Care Equipment			
Major Appliances			
Musical Equipment			
Out Door Equipment			
Weapons/Hunting			

About Your – Net Worth Statement

A net worth statement provides an overall financial picture. List your assets, list your obligations, and subtract the debts from the assets.

NET WORTH STATEMENT as of _______________

ASSETS	
Cash on Hand	$____________
Bank Accounts (Checking and Savings)	$____________
Savings & Loan Accounts	$____________
Any Other Savings Accounts	$____________
House, Market Value	$____________
Other Real Estate, Value	$____________
Household Furnishings, Value	$____________
Vehicles Blue Book Value	$____________
Life Insurance, Cash Value	$____________
Stocks and Bonds, Today's Value	$____________
Profit-Sharing or Retirement Plans	$____________
U.S. Savings Bonds	$____________
Money Owed to You	$____________
Other Assets or Investments	$____________
Personal Property	$____________
TOTAL ASSETS	$____________
DEBTS	
Mortgages, Balance Due	$____________
Other Loans (Bank, Credit Union)	$____________
Installment Debts, Balance Due	$____________
Credit Cards, Balance Due	$____________
Charge Accounts, Owed	$____________
Other Debts, Total Owed	$____________
Insurance Premiums Due	$____________
Taxes Owed	$____________
Vehicles Loans	$____________
Other Current Bills	$____________
TOTAL DEBTS	$____________
NET WORTH (Assets Minus Debts)	$____________

Personal Notes

Acknowledgments

I live an authentic life because of my family – my greatest blessing. I thank my mother *Mami*, for her insight, my children for their encouragement and love, my partner Joel *my Papí*, for his patience, understanding and willingness to always feed me.

To my wonderful – and best – support group Janny, Toni, Camille, Evelyn, Heather, Leah, Lydia, my LPhiD's – SSH – and Domingo Sabroso crew, Thank you!

Special thank you to J.L. Lora, a fantastic author of great romance novels. I appreciate the inspiration, advice and the countless humor-filled lively discussions. Find her at www.JLLora.com.

My family and my friends allow me to express and exist on so many different planes. They understand my need to balance my creative, and artistic expressions with logical linear thinking, and a ready smile.

With gratitude, as always – Peace and Love.

About the Author

O. Escobar is Puerto Rican American author. She earned a Masters of Arts Degree in Organizational Management, and a Bachelor's of Arts Degree in Legal Studies and American Studies. She is an executive editor, a contemporary abstract painter and metal sculptor. She contributes her time, resources, and talents to a not for profit organizations. She lives in Maryland with her family and her dog Billy. Find her at www.oescobar.org, on Twitter @OEscobarArtist, and on Facebook at www.facebook.com/ OEscobarArtist

Disclaimer

The Your True Order Guide to Gathering, Organizing and Storing Your Personal Records is not a substitute for personalized legal advice from an accredited and knowledgeable legal attorney licensed to practice in your State. The information provided is not legal advice. The material is written with an international audience in mind, and not specific to the applicable laws and regulations in any individual country or economic entity. No external materials, or any intellectual properties of others, are used, or intended to be used.

Your True Order makes no warranty, expressed or implied, as to the results obtained from the use of the information. We have no liability for the accuracy of the information and are not liable for any third-party claims or losses of any damages. The user shall have the right to view the information and usage for the purpose intended, and disclosed.

Use of Trademark in stylized or modified form of our logo and product names permitted under license only – unauthorized use strictly prohibited.

Copyright

Copyright © 2017 O. Escobar /Your True Order - All Rights Reserved.

"All rights reserved," indicates that the copyright holder reserves, or holds for their own use, all the rights provided by copyright law under one specific copyright treaty. The intellectual property/publication or any portion thereof, may not be reproduced, distributed, or transmitted in any form or by any means, including: photocopying, recording, or other electronic or mechanical methods, without the prior written permission of the publisher, except in the case of brief quotations embodied in critical reviews and certain other noncommercial uses permitted by copyright law. For permission requests, write to the publisher, addressed "Attention: Permissions Coordinator," at the address below.

O. Escobar /Your True Order
PO Box 47022
Windsor Mill, MD 21244
www.oescobar.org

Made in the USA
Monee, IL
05 November 2026

67377169R00105